WELCOME TO BETWS-Y-COED
THE STORY OF A SNOWDONIA VILLAGE

First edition: 2004
New edition: 2013

ISBN: 978-1-84527-454-2

Cover design: Carreg Gwalch

Published by Gwasg Carreg Gwalch,
12 Iard yr Orsaf, Llanrwst, Wales LL26 0EH
tel: 01492 642031
fax: 01492 641502
email: books@carreg-gwalch.com
website: www.carreg-gwalch.com

The Royal Oak on the A5 at Betws-y-coed

Pont Soldiwrs ('Soldiers' bridge')

Carreg Gwalch Guides

Welcome to
Betws-y-coed

The Story of a Snowdonia Village
by Catrin Mair

Contents

A map of the Conwy Valley   6

Introduction   8

Celtic roots   11

Bronze, Iron and Lead   15

Llanfihangel y Betws   19

Rebel country   23

A Welsh Bible for all in the land   27

'The drovers are coming!'   31

River crossings and bridges   35

Falls and fairies   39

Fishing the mountain waters   43

The lakes of Betws-y-coed   47

The A5 – a historic route   51

The Artists' Village   55

Gethin Jones – master builder   59

Mines, quarries and forests   63

From crafts to craft shops   67

A walk around Betws-y-coed   76

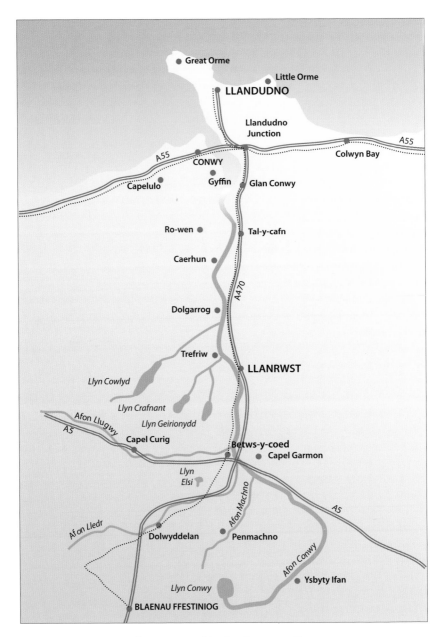

Betws-y-coed in the Conwy valley

Afon Llugwy in the centre of the village

The Swallow Falls Hotel

Introduction

A village for all seasons

Whether the peaks of Eryri are white with snow, draped in autumn colours, under mist and rain, or bright and clear on a summer afternoon, Betws-y-coed will be full of life. The village and the Conwy Valley offers the ideal base for a leisurely walk or relaxing day out in the mountains. A newcomer would be forgiven for thinking the whole place was invented for the tourist trade. Its quality shops and galleries, its attractive cafes and restaurants and riverside setting have a magnetism which visitors find hard to resist. In fact, the heart of the village is not that old and new developments are witnessed annually. But if the place has evolved over the years, thanks to the locals, it has not lost its charm or rich inheritance. For there is so much more to Betws-y-coed than meets the eye.

Summer greens in the woodlands around Betws-y-coed

A winter scene

Autumn colours in the village

Dinas Mawr above the A5 to the south-east of Betws-y-coed

Cwm Wybrnant, between Dolwyddelan and Penmachno

Celtic roots

Wales has an oral mythical tradition which stretches back to the Ice Age. The Welsh language has maintained this unbroken link with the legends of the Celtic past. Every mountain, lake and river has a story to tell.

To the south-east of Betws-y-coed, the A5 descends suddenly down a craggy slope. This hill is called Dinas Mawr – *dinas* is a common name in Wales and it usually signifies a hill-top fort from the Iron Age. In modern Welsh, it means 'city'. These forts were established during the centuries when Celtic tribes crossed from central and southern Europe and set up villages along the Welsh coast, before gradually inhabiting the upland valleys.

Dragons were believed to hang out in wild and inhospitable terrain and it isn't surprising that the upper Conwy valley has its fair share of dragon legends. Historically, they were described as huge flying adders – *gwiber* in Welsh. The upland valley of Wybrnant lies a few miles south of Betws-y-coed, called 'Wibernant' apparently, after the dragon that lived there. Legend has it that many a brave man tried in vain to rid the *ardal* of its terror, and that the dragon gathered up their bones.

In nearby St Gwyddelan church, Dolwyddelan, an old oak beam (probably from an earlier church) carries a carving of a sea dragon which swam upriver and was later dragged to a mountain lake. This is believed to be a reference to the water monster – the *afanc* (*afanc* also means 'beaver') – which lived beneath the eerie, peat-black, still waters of Llyn yr Afanc where the rivers Conwy and Lledr converge half a mile upstream from Betws-y-coed. At one time the *afanc* wreaked havoc among the early inhabitants of the valley. His skin was so tough; no arrow or spear could pierce it. They hatched a plan and the huge monster was charmed out of the dark waters by a beautiful maiden. It was chained and hooked to the strongest pair of oxen in the land. They then dragged the *afanc* up the valley past Dolwyddelan, up Bwlch Rhiw'r Ychen ('ox-hill pass') until one of the oxen had strained so much that its eye fell out. Hence the aptly named lake, Pwll Llygad yr Ych ('ox-eye pool'). Finally the monster was let loose in Llyn Cwm Ffynnon Las, one of the high mountain lakes of Eryri (*Snowdonia*).

Many other legends and myths have prevailed – a number of them recording adventures related to specific places and evoking wild and wonderful explanations of place-names. But the greatest Celtic heritage here is the Welsh language itself, without which the legends would be meaningless. After centuries of oppression and decline, the language is once again thriving. It is adapting to the challenges of a new era, yet remains to this day a rich reservoir of words and culture, connecting us across the centuries to our Celtic ancestry.

Llyn yr Afanc, on Afon Conwy – in two different seasons

The dragon carving in Dolwyddelan's church

St Gwyddelan's church, Dolwyddelan

The chambered tomb – Cromlech Capel Garmon

The location of the Roman fort on the meadows near Capel Curig

Bronze, Iron and Lead

The village of Capel Garmon lies east of Betws-y-coed above the Conwy valley. Beyond the village is Cromlech Capel Garmon – a megalithic chambered tomb, regarded as one of the finest examples of a passage grave in the British Isles. Beaker pottery was found here which appears to have been still in use in the Bronze Age. The *cromlech* is estimated to be 4,000 years old – a thousand years old when the Celts arrived, two millennia old when the Romans came and over three thousand years old at the time of the Norman and Saxon invasion. A bronze spear was unearthed near another *cromlech* in the area, and a Celtic iron fire-dog in a peat bog on a nearby farm. This is now displayed at the National Museum of Wales in Cardiff.

The Romans had forts at Caerhun near the Conwy estuary and Caer Llugwy near Capel Curig. They had villas at Deganwy and fished for mussel pearls in the river. At the time, Afon Conwy was world famous for its pearls. The last one to be discovered in its shell was in 1955. The Romans ignored the low marshes of the valley floors and paved their roads on the brows of the hills and through the mountain passes.

Their most famous road in Wales was called Sarn Elen, after a Welsh princess from Caernarfon who married a Roman governor. Sarn Elen followed the upland route from Caerhun south towards Trawsfynydd, where there was a large camp at Tomen y Mur during the Roman occupation. Parts of the road's embankments are still visible, although the original pavements and stonework are now hidden under turf and soil.

Sarn Elen crossed Afon Llugwy at Pont y Mwynwyr (*Miners' Bridge*) near Betws-y-coed. In AD78, the armies of Agricola set up camp near the river between Tŷ Hyll and Capel Curig, and fortified it with a timber wall. They stayed and re-built an 8-acre stone transit camp, complete with hot and cold baths. It heralded the Betws-y-coed tradition of hospitality and good accommodation –

and left much broken pottery to the joy of later archaeologists.

The site was excavated in 1920 and named Caer Llugwy, since the original Roman name had been lost. Traces of the settlement can still be seen on Bryn Gefeiliau farm. The Romans maintained a thriving mining industry in the area – they opened and worked lead mines in the surrounding hills and there was a large community here for three centuries. Excavations have disclosed substantial pillared buildings and vast halls, suggesting the presence of a local governor of some significance. The beauty of the valley, the wealth in its rocks and the confluence of roads were no doubt contributory factors in the choice of location.

Miners' Bridge

Rhiwddolion and the Roman foundations of Sarn Elen

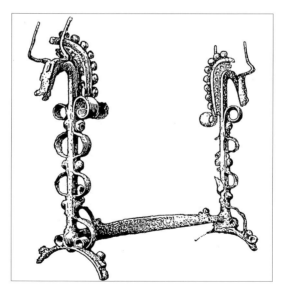

The old Celtic fire-dog found in a peat marsh near Capel Garmon

The old church of 'Llanfihangel y Betws'

Llanfihangel y Betws

The hamlet now known as Llanfihangel was once called Betws Wyrion Iddon, the chapel of the grandchildren of Iddon, and was a part of the parish of Llanrhychwyn, above Llanrwst. Iddon was the owner of the land where the original chapel stood. The current name of the existing church near the railway station is Eglwys Sant Mihangel (*St Michael's*) and in the 16th century a separate parish was created here, known as Llanfihangel y Betws. The church name must have been in use for some time, however, since dedicating churches to Mihangel was the custom of the Celtic Church before Vatican influence.

Eglwys Sant Mihangel is splendidly situated above the pools of Afon Conwy. Its peaceful churchyard is characterised by ancient vast yew trees and an abundance of wild flowers. It has two lych-gates – including one built in 1756 on the western side, a number of table tombs and old gravestones (dating as far back as 1696), now resting against the walls of the church itself.

The nave and chancel of the long narrow church are 14th century. It was preceeded by an earlier building, which probably housed the 12th century font still found inside. A north transept was added in 1843, along with new windows which incorporated fragments of earlier stained glass, but the wooden altar, pulpit and reading desk are 17th century.

A finely-carved effigy of an armoured knight is found in the chancel. The Welsh/Latin inscription tells us that here lies Gruffudd, son of Dafydd Goch (*the Red*), the great, great grandson of Llywelyn Fawr. Gruffudd was a knight who lived at Fedw Deg, on the southern side of Afon Lledr, and his effigy is presented in studded armour, in the style of the second half of the 14th century. He was the father of Hywel Coetmor and Rhys Gethin, local Welsh warriors who were leading men in Owain Glyndŵr's fight for freedom.

The church was at one time used as a village school and the

intriguing score marks on the south-west and north-west angles of the nave, are evidence of the popularity of ball games in the old churchyard.

The gravestones in Llanfihangel are rich in the 4 line classical Welsh epitaph stanzas called *englyn*. Old Welsh manuscripts suggest that the englyn had already become a written form of poetry by the 8th century. The earliest recorded gravestone inscription however is 1725. It is especially pleasing to find an englyn on Elin Gruffydd's stone (near the southern entrance), dated 1737. The last two lines capture the spirit of the place: '*Mewn glyn nefawl ynglan afon/A llath o bridd yn llethu i bron*' ('She lies in a heavenly valley by the river/With a yard of earth on her breast'). These epitaphs were written by traditional local poets practising the ancient craft of the bards of the Welsh princes, weaving music into words in a complex art form still alive today.

The effigy of Gruffudd ap Dafydd Goch

The epitaph of a cattle drover

An old yew in the churchyard

Dolwyddelan castle

Rebel country

Dolwyddelan castle, a few miles up Dyffryn Lledr, is typical of the Welsh strongholds: deep in rugged terrain, standing on a craggy rock, using a steep cliff as natural fortification. It was built in the 13th century and commands extensive views of the surrounding territory. Llywelyn Fawr (*the Great*) is believed to have been born in Dolwyddelan in an earlier castle located a short distance from the present site.

His grandsons, Llywelyn and Dafydd ap Gruffudd, became *Tywysogion Cymru* (Princes of Wales) and continued the powerful struggle for their country. Dolwyddelan, stark and strategic, controlled mountain passes and links with comrades in southern territories. Unlike the English, the *Cymry* (Welsh people) held on to their independence for over two centuries after the Battle of Hastings, but the sheer number, wealth and resources of the invading armies overwhelmed their defending forces in 1282. Llywelyn was killed in a skirmish in mid Wales, Edward I's huge army crossed Afon Conwy near Betws-y-coed and captured Dolwyddelan castle and Dafydd was hung, drawn and quartered on Shrewsbury's Pride Hill – the first person to experience that particularly barbaric form of execution.

Eryri, the mountain fortress, was never really subjugated – Edward prefered the safety of his coastal castles and his sea escape routes. The upper valleys of Conwy, Llugwy, Lledr and Machno became a bandit country which English officials and colonists from the new garrison towns would not dare enter.

The 14th century saw tensions build between the *Cymry*, enslaved in their own lands without any citizens' rights, and the foreign townspeople with their preferential marketing rights. In 1400 discontent escalated into a full-scale War of Independence led by the national hero of Wales, Owain Glyndŵr. Every castle in Wales was attacked and put under siege; every new borough was burnt. Even Conwy town and castle fell to the lightly armed Welsh forces and by 1405, nearly the whole of Wales was under Owain's control.

These valleys, as expected, raised faithful followers for Glyndŵr's campaign. Two local brothers, Hywel Coetmor and Rhys Gethin, with Welsh princes' blood in their veins, were among his most prominent military leaders. Hywel Coetmor was the first known owner of Castell Gwydir, near Llanrwst and had captained a hundred Denbighshire men on Poitiers' battlefield in France. His stone effigy lies in Capel Gwydir, Llanrwst church. Rhys Gethin ('the fierce') is connected with Cwmlannerch farm near Betws-y-coed and Hendre Rhys Gethin, Pentre-du. He masterminded Glyndŵr's most sweeping victory in open battle, *brwydr* Bryn Glas in 1402. Both were highly praised by the most eminent poets of their age.

Hywel Coetmor's effigy at Llanrwst

Capel Gwydir, Llanrwst church

Hendre Rhys Gethin farmhouse, Betws-y-coed

Tŷ Mawr Wybrnant, near Penmachno

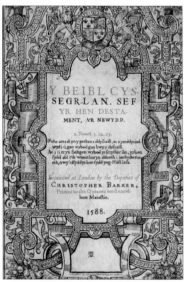

Bishop William Morgan and his printed Welsh Bible

A Welsh Bible for all in the land

When the so-called Act of Union, annexed *Cymru* into the English state in 1536, the Welsh language was prohibited from all official proceedings and documents. With the Reformation, the new English Bible was enthroned in every church – and for the Welsh congregations was even more foreign than the Latin scriptures.

For a thousand years, *Cymraeg* (Welsh) had been the language of royalty, officialdom and the law courts of the land, as well as the language of the common people. The Welsh monks had recorded one of the oldest literatures of Europe on their stylish parchments.

By 1534, Martin Luther and his colleagues had finished their model German translation of the Bible. Wales, like most other European countries, came under its influence, and spiritual leaders called for a Welsh version of the Scriptures. There were also political considerations. With the Reformation came a real danger of revolt in Ireland and the threat of Spanish invasion. Wales provided a possible gateway to an army to march onwards to England. One way of ensuring the loyalty of the Welsh people to the Protestant cause would be to translate the Bible into Welsh.

Queen Elizabeth I, herself hailing from Anglesey gentry, bowed to the demands of the spiritual leaders and the dictates of policy and commissioned the bishops of Wales and Hereford to produce a Welsh translation, which was to be used in every church in Wales. The first person to translate the whole Bible into Welsh was William Morgan from Tŷ Mawr Wybrnant, which lies in a beautiful secluded valley between Penmachno and Dyffryn Lledr. This is now a National Trust property, restored to its probable 16th-17th century appearance. It houses a display of bibles in several languages and traditional Welsh furniture. The site also includes a nature trail .

Bishop William Morgan's Welsh Bible was published in 1588 and became an instant classic. It drew on the essence of traditional Welsh literature to create a beautiful modern prose and hailed the beginning of the renaissance of the language, a process which continues today: 'His work is the rock on which the present Welsh language is so strongly built. It marks the appearance of a cohesive standard language, Modern Welsh.' (Michael Senior, *Portrait of North Wales*, 2001)

Two other Welsh scholars who helped with the work, Richard Davies and William Salesbury, were also from Dyffryn Conwy, this *ardal* being a bastion of the Welsh literary and poetic tradition during the Rennaissance. Later reformations in the 18th and 19th centuries saw nonconformist denominations establishing their congregations in the vicinity of Betws-y-coed – originally in farmhouses, and later, in chapels. These were thoroughly Welsh, promoting cultural meetings (*eisteddfodau*) and publishing books and periodicals, as well as day to day religious activities.

A collection of different editions of the Welsh Bible inside Tŷ Mawr Wybrnant

The hearth, Tŷ Mawr Wybrnant

An old nonconformist chapel at Betws-y-coed

'Welsh Drovers' by H. Tennent

Smithfield Market, London

'The drovers are coming!'

From the late Middle Ages to the coming of the railways, thousands of herds of cattle, sheep, pigs and flocks of geese were driven eastwards from the hill pastures of Wales to the fattening grounds and rich markets of England. The Welsh drovers herded their stock hundreds of miles, usually over difficult mountain terrain, long before the New World cowboys weaved their romantic myths about life in the saddle.

Dyffryn Conwy and its tributary valleys are excellent grazing grounds and it is not surprising that many prominent drovers and their hands were born and bred here. The Welsh term *porthmon* is used to describe the powerful livestock dealers and the term *gyrrwr* to describe the able hand that helped to walk the animals to England. They were the natural professions of the *ardal*.

At one time in the 18th century, records show that there were 6 *porthmyn* in each of the small, local upland villages of Penmachno, Ysbyty Ifan and Dolwyddelan. Every *porthmon* would probably hire 6 - 10 hands to drive their herds as far as Kent.

Drovers by and large, had a bad image. Moving from tavern to tavern between dawn and dusk, some were notorious drunkards and brawlers. English landlords were said to take down curtains and raise whatever carpets they had if they heard the Welsh drovers were heading for town. Some were rogues and cheaters, and one or two vanished to Ireland with their takings.

In general, however, they were honest, if hard, and were renowned for straight-dealing. At the time, they were essential to the Welsh rural economy and were known as the 'Welsh Armada', bringing the gold home. They were entrusted annually with every smallholder's stock and were only granted the special porthmon licence if they were over thirty, married and owned a house.

The respect for the profession is manifested in the inscription on one of the oldest gravestones in Llanfihangel y Betws. Hardly any other profession is acknowledged on the tombs, but on the northern wall of the church there is a stone with the inscription: 'Yma y mae yn gorwedd gorph Evan Thomas y porthmon a gladdwyd yn y flwyddyn 1747' ('Here lies the body of Evan Thomas the drover, buried in 1747') along with the traditional Welsh tribute: an epitaph *englyn* in the strict metres (see page 19).

Evan Thomas, and other Dyffryn Conwy *porthmyn* would have driven their stock from the markets of Llanrwst, over the hills to Betws-yn-Rhos and onwards to St Asaph and Chester or from Ysbyty Ifan, using the high roads, to Wrexham. On crossing the border, they would have followed some of the numerous paths still called 'Welsh Roads' or 'Welsh Ways' into the heart of England.

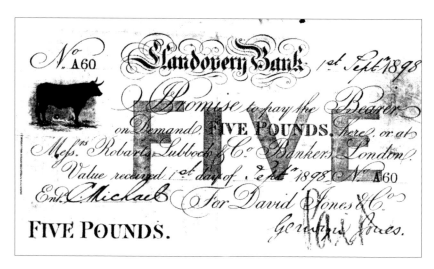

A £5 note by a Welsh Drover Bank

An Anglesey ox – a a typical hardy breed of Welsh Black cattle

An early scene at Betws-y-coed

Pont-ar-Ledr, built by Hywel y Saer

Pont-y-pair

River crossings and bridges

Betws-y-coed is at a grand junction of three rivers: **Lledr**, flowing down from Dolwyddelan and Moel Siabod; **Llugwy**, the white-water descending from Capel Curig, Llynnau Mymbyr and the Carneddau mountains, and **Conwy**, the valley's largest river, from its source in Llyn Conwy above Ysbyty Ifan to its estuary near Conwy town. As all three narrow valleys descend rapidly towards the village, it is hardly surprising that every possible river crossing was valued and that the area has produced a high degree of interest and skill in the art of bridge building.

Downstream from the railway at Betws-y-coed, an old ford is referred to in the name Rhydycreuau on the opposite bank of Afon Conwy (*rhyd*, ford; *creuau*, pigsties;). At that point, the remains of stepping stones can still be seen clearly – they were once important to parishoners coming to worship in the old church.

An interesting pedestrian bridge can be found at the back of the old church. It is now an iron suspension bridge, cast in 1930, to replace a temporary wooden structure built by sappers during World War I, but swept away by a flood in 1928. The new bridge is still called '*Pont Soldiwrs*' by local people.

In the mid 15th century, Hywel y Saer (the mason) was travelling to Conwy from Y Bala when he came across a flood on the banks of Afon Lledr, near its confluence with Afon Conwy. He stayed there and built a bridge of his own accord, without asking payment from anybody who crossed it, save what they wished to give him. The bridge, called Pont-ar-Ledr, still stands today and serves the community.

He repeated this feat on the banks of Afon Llugwy, building the beautiful arched bridge of Pont-y-pair around 1475. The dramatic, frothing cauldron that gave the bridge its name can be viewed downstream from the bridge. A second bridge was built upstream on convenient rocks alongside the first, but slightly out of alignment, giving the combined bridge a total of 11 arches, all with different sizes and spans.

Further upstream stands Pont y Mwynwyr ('miners' bridge'), built originally by the miners of Pentre-du as a short-cut to cross Afon Llugwy to the lead mines in the hills. It is a solid wooden structure, built on the site of an old Roman crossing where the Roman road, Sarn Elen, crossed the valley on its way from Caerhun, near Conwy to Tomen y Mur, near Trawsfynydd. It is a fascinating structure and looks like a ship's gangway spanning the lower southern bank and the higher rocks on the northern side.

An old engraving of Pont-y-pair

Pont Soldiwrs across Afon Conwy

Pont y Mwynwyr   *Pont Soldiwrs*

The falls on Afon Llugwy

A famous landmark at Betws-y-coed

Falls and fairies

The wonderful cataract of seething white water on Afon Llugwy is something that all visitors to Betws-y-coed came to admire. There is some confusion about its proper name. In Welsh, it is very aptly called Rhaeadr Ewynnol, the foaming falls, but someone somwhere misinterpreted *Ewynnol* for *Y wennol*, 'the swallow'. Visitors have ever since looked in vain for a swallow shape in its splendid rock and foam formation!

Sight-seers have been paying since the mid-19th century for the privilege of seeing the spectacle. At one time, horse-drawn cars waited on the station platform offering to take daytrippers back and forth. The best view is from a convenient concrete platform at the bottom of a flight of steps descending from the A5. It is truly dramatic, but hard to catch through a camera lens due to the constant spray from the three-stepped falls.

According to the legend, a local aristocrat is responsible for the moaning sound of the waterfall. Sir John Wynn of Castell Gwydir, near Llanrwst, was a land-grabbing scoundrel. His spirit has been in purgatory beneath the water since 1627, in an attempt to wash away his long list of earthly sins.

Following Afon Conwy upstream from Waterloo bridge will bring you eventually to a long and deep gorge, called Ffos Noddyn. It has since time immemorial been associated in Welsh legends with fairies, as it seems like a natural entrance to the Celtic underworld of *Annwn* with its strange and fascinating characters. Victorian visitors hearing these tales nicknamed the place 'Fairy Glen'. The combination of rapids and cascades, the steep rock formations on either side of the narrow ravine and the impressive play of sunshine and shadows on its wooded banks all add to its charm.

White water river sports enthusiasts are drawn to canoe and float the wild rivers and gorges of Betws-y-coed, a pastime which is best left to the strictly professional because of the unpredictable nature of the waters. Further upstream, Afon Conwy plunges down yet another waterfall, known as Rhaeadr y Graig Lwyd. The foot of this cascade used to be the highest point that the leaping Atlantic salmon could climb to find its spawning grounds after the long journey back from Greenland. In the middle of the falls, there are the remains of a man-made salmon ladder which tried to open new territories for the salmon – and the anglers! – in the upper valleys. After two failed attempts (the last of which was in 1860), a 50 m tunnel, 5 m in diameter, consisting of 28 resting pools was succesfully bored through the rock in 1993. It is predicted that this will lead to a 20% increase in the valley's fish stock.

Ffos Noddyn ('Fairy Glen')

The salmon ladder at Rhaeadr y Graig Lwyd

White water sport near Betws-y-coed

John Jones, Tanrallt in his Conwy river coracle

Traditional salmon traps on Afon Lledr

Fishing the mountain waters

Wild trout and salmon have graced the tables of these valleys since the earliest dwellers settled here. Over the centuries, a profusion of methods and inventions were developed to catch fish on different sections of the river. As one local historian puts it:

> 'The old inhabitants of Nant Conwy possessed fishing skills the likes of which had not been seen, as far as I know, beyond that region. Although various strangers happened to call from time to time, and amongst them the fisheries' representatives, one and all proclaimed that they had never seen such original equipment and instruments as the fishing coracles, nets, chests and baskets of the upper reaches of Nant Conwy.'

Coracles have been used in Wales since Celtic times and although they are now limited by licence to three rivers in the south-west, at one time they were employed on all Welsh rivers provided the pools were wide and quiet enough. In 1914, John Jones of Tanrallt, Dyffryn Lledr was the last of a long line of local coracle fishermen to fish Llyn yr Afanc. When his father and others worked the pools from coracles, they used sturdy poles, several yards in length, to disturb the water in the corners and crevices where the salmon hid, so as to drive the fish into the nets which had been placed across their runs, in the river bed. John Jones' coracle is now in Amgueddfa Werin Cymru (*the Museum of Welsh Life*), Sain Ffagan, outside Cardiff.

In places where the rivers are wilder and the beds rockier, nets – some made of local rushes – were placed in natural gaps and crevices to catch the fish. 'Chests' and 'V'-shaped baskets were made of hazelwood sticks and fashioned so as to slot exactly into the bed that had been carved in the rock by the flow of the water. The basket was made by hand to fill the bed, whatever shape or size it might be, and the salmon fell into the basket in the ravine while attempting to jump the falls. The baskets had to be renewed every two years. Only one fisherman is licensed to use a basket on Afon Lledr today – these ancient fishing methods, here since the dawn of time, are being slowly eroded away.

In Victorian times, fishing as a sport rather than a necessity became increasingly popular and Betws-y-coed thrived on its natural resources. The Atlantic salmon is a magnificent fish and wild rivers like Conwy, Llugwy and Lledr offer fascinating sightings of the leaping salmon on its way to the spawning grounds after a 2,000-mile return swim from Greenland. Various stretches of the rivers were bought by anglers' clubs and in 1961, the Betws-y-coed Anglers' Club was founded to control permits for all fishing on its Conwy and Llugwy waters, as well as on three lakes in the vicinity.

The record rod and line catch on Afon Conwy was a 46lb (21kg) male salmon, 4ft 2ins (127cm) long, caught in the Wall Pool (Llyn Wal) near the railway bridge, Pont-troed-yr-afon, and landed after a 2 hour struggle by a local Llanrwst man in November 1892.

A Conwy salmon on display in a Betws-y-coed bar

Fishing at Llyn Crafnant

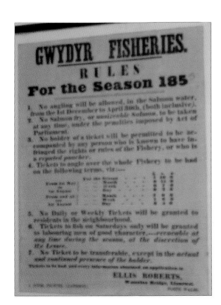

Past heritage of Betws' anglers

Llyn Elsi

Llyn Parc

The lakes of Betws-y-coed

There are many lakes in the hills that surround the village – two within fairly easy walking distance.

LLYN ELSI, situated at 223 m in the uplands between the Llugwy and Lledr valleys provide the village with its water supply. It is stocked with American brook trout and brown trout and its fishing rights are controlled by Betws-y-coed Anglers' Club. As the crow flies, it is only half a mile from the A5, but there is a maze of trails through the woods to reach it. The easiest path starts behind St Mary's Church. The lake itself is on a magnificent plateau with a panoramic view of Moel Siabod and Eryri. The shores are free of plantation, with the native bracken and birch framing its coves and islets with colour, even in winter.

LLYN PARC at 202 m, is another popular walking destination. Today, it is almost entirely surrounded by forestry plantation but it was used in the past as a reservoir for water power for the mines below. Other lead mines higher up the slopes have contaminated the lake's waters and there are no fish here. The dam has deteriorated over the years and now the sluice is left open so that the water level is kept low. The copper/lead/zinc in the rocks has given the lake a high mineral content and an alpine greenish colour. In autumn, when the bracken and the sedges turn orange and russet, the lake looks strangely beautiful.

LLYN GODDIONDUON and **LLYN BYCHAN** are situated to the north west of the village and are stocked with brown trout. They can be approached by a path through the forestry plantations above Glyn Farm, about a mile from Tŷ Hyll ('the ugly house').

LLYN BODGYNYDD, and its connected lake **LLYN BODGYNYDD BACH**, lies in the same part of the forest. Fishing rights for these two, and also for nearby Llyn Glangors, belong to the Llanrwst Angling Club.

Outside the immediate vicinity of Betws-y-coed, many other bright and enchanting lakes merit a visit. **LLYNNAU MYMBYR** above Capel Curig is one of the most photogenic in Wales with the Wyddfa, Carnedd Ugain, Crib Goch and Lliwedd ('Snowdon horseshoe') as its dramatic backdrop.

Deeper into the Gwydir forest lie **LLYN GEIRIONYDD** and **LLYN CRAFNANT**, both accessible by car. Llyn Geirionydd is polluted by its mines and disturbed by water skiers and jet-skis but is a peaceful haven once the crowds have left. Llyn Crafnant has a lakeside café, which also hires boats and sells fishing permits.

The lakes of Betws-y-coed are shy waters, and are not easily found. This, however, has largely guarded their privacy and the persevering traveller is thoroughly rewarded.

Llynnau Mymbyr in winter

Llyn Geirionydd

Llyn Crafnant

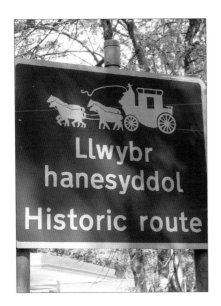

The A5 at Betws-y-coed and a Telford milestone

Lord Penrhyn's road above Capel Curig

The A5 – a historic route

Until the late eighteenth century, Betws-y-coed was a tiny hamlet centred around the corn mill in Pentre-felin.

Pack-horse tracks and an old stone bridge served to connect it to the wider world. A road system was needed to speed up the mail and the transport of government officials between London and Dublin. At the time, it was a laborious 45-hour coach ride from London to Holyhead – over the hills from Shrewsbury to Llanrwst, reaching Conwy and then along the coast.

In 1791-2, Lord Penrhyn – following an election defeat at the hands of the burghers of Conwy – swore revenge on the town and opened a new section of road above Capel Curig, along with a grand new inn, the Royal Hotel (now Plas y Brenin). After the 1800 Act of Union with Ireland, this shorter route through the mountains of Eryri was favoured, causing havoc to Conwy merchants.

The Irish Mail coach switched to the Betws-y-coed route, making the village the gateway to Eryri ever since. The present Pont yr Afanc (*Beaver Bridge*) has a wonderful semi-circular arch and was built upstream from Betws-y-coed at the lower end of the Conwy gorge. A smithy and new coaching inns were built. Thomas Telford submitted a report commissioned by parliament in 1811 and called for further improvement to what is now the A5.

Work commenced and Telford cut an entirely new road into the Dinas hill rockface and in 1815 built the bridge across Afon Conwy: the Waterloo bridge. The bridge has a cast-iron structure from a Shrewsbury foundry and is still called Y Bont Haearn ('the Iron Bridge') in Welsh. The bridge's spandrels contain the four national emblems of the countries of these isles: the Welsh leek, Ireland's shamrock, the Scottish thistle and England's rose. It was indeed a route of international significance.

In 1749, the parish population was only 200. By 1884, after Telford's creations and the arrival in 1868 of the steam train, the population had grown to almost 800. The village boasted 6 licensed hotels – Glan Aber, Gwydyr, Miners Arms, Royal Oak, Swan (now renamed Pont-y-pair) and Waterloo. There were 5 temperance houses, together with 34 boarding houses, a post office, a draper, 2 tailors, 4 grocers, a chemist, a bootmaker and 2 coal merchants.

The Royal Oak kept 23 horses and 12 traps for hire, and four-in-hand trips were arranged from Llandudno to Betws-y-coed, up to Rhaeadr Ewynnol and around the mountain lakes of Eryri. A reminder of this bustle is the horse watering-trough filled with summer flowers outside St Mary's Church.

'Y Bont Haearn' – Waterloo bridge, 1815

Detail of the Welsh leek, Waterloo bridge

The Royal Oak – a coaching inn at Betws-y-coed

'The Valley of Dolwyddelan' by George Popkin, c. 1816

'A Welsh funeral' located at the old church, Betws-y-coed, by David Cox

The Artists' Village

Many travellers visiting Betws-y-coed today will have bought a painting, a print, some pottery, slate craft or wood carving. Its environment still inspires craftspeople and artists and allows them to flourish.

It was the bridge and road builders who first opened these upland valleys to passing travellers, but it was the painters that followed who drew the world's attention to the beauty of its rugged landscape. During the first part of the 19th century, the small houses and inns of the parish were inundated with artists – they came for the summer months and some built their own houses, giving the grander buildings a touch of the alpine architecture they had seen on their travels.

These included prolific landscape artists such as Henry Gastineau (1791-1876), George Pickering (1794-1857) and probably the best known of all, David Cox (1785-1859). Although born in Birmingham, Cox spent so much time in Betws-y-coed that he was regarded as a Welsh artist. He first visited in 1844, staying at the Royal Oak – then a small whitewashed inn. He returned every summer until 1856, turning the village into an open-air studio. He painted all the famous pools, bridges and old cottages of the *ardal*, including a new sign for the Royal Oak itself. One of his most famous paintings is 'A Welsh Funeral' (1848) which depicted the burial of the landlord's daughter, shortly before sunset, according to the custom of rural Wales at the time. When Cox died in 1859, he was still a little known painter of everyday life, an impressionist before his time, but he had captured Betws-y-coed in all shades of wind and weather.

Betws-y-coed became more famous than David Cox, but owes its fame to the artist. The Royal Oak was rebuilt and the village became a popular beauty spot, especially for honeymooners. Victorian tourists arrived in their thousands, with their fishing rods, walking sticks and painting easels.

This was how it was portrayed in *The Art Journal* (1894):
'Betws-y-coed is one of the resting places for those of artistic temperament. At some time or another, every artist and every art-lover has been there, if only for a single day. Since David Cox made it his chief resort, more than fifty years ago, Betws-y-coed has steadily increased in artistic fame. All the waterfalls have been painted, every valley has had its masterpiece, and almost every rock can be found in one picture or another.'

A beech wood above Pentre-du was painted to exhaustion and became known as Artist's Wood. Artists wrote lyrically about the grandeur that overpowered them. A careful homage has been paid to these painters in Peter Lord's fine volume *The Betws-y-coed Artists' Colony 1844-1914.*

Peter Lord's history of Betws' artists

Some of today's craft shops and galeries at Betws-y-coed

The station building built by Gethin Jones at Betws-y-coed

St Mary's church

Gethin Jones – master builder

The growth of Betws-y-coed and the requirements of a new Victorian era called for an army of house and railroad builders. Local quarries often provided the raw materials and local craftsmen adapted well to the needs of the age. A local carpenter, Owen Gethin Jones from the parish of Penmachno, became a large-scale entrepreneur and master builder.

Born in 1816, he started working at the age of 12 with little formal education. He benefitted however from being brought up in a Welsh community. He learnt the poet's craft and became a published local historian. In the 1860's the railway advanced up Dyffryn Conwy and Gethin built the Queens Hotel and the station in Llanrwst. He completed Betws-y-coed station in 1868 at a cost of nearly £8,000.

As Betws-y-coed expanded, the existing church became too small to contain its growing number of parishioners. A new building was commissioned for £5,000, with Charles Kurts of Coed Celyn contributing most of the money. Gethin took the contract and built the beautifully crafted St Mary's church on part of Cae Llan (the village fairground), It was completed in 1873, but the project cost Gethin dearly and he made a loss of £400. He was so dismayed that, according to local legend, for the rest of his life, every time he passed the building, he turned his head the other way, so as not be reminded of its poor financial management. The spacious well-luminated church with its lovely interior of local blue stone and Ancaster sandstone is however a fitting testimony to his craft.

The railroad was heading to Ffestiniog and Gethin started work on the Dyffryn Lledr viaduct – a quarter mile long stone masterpiece which immortalizes his name. The builder visited Köln in Germany and studied the huge cathedral there and the magnificent Rhine bridges; he also drew on Castell Dolwyddelan for inspiration. The finished viaduct has castellated piers and parapet walls of local stone, with the mortar kept back from the wall face to maintain its traditional character. Gethin was an environmentalist ahead of his time and his 7 arches (31 of the original arches have been closed) are in harmony with the valley's wild terrain. The largest arch spans 182ft (55 m) and stands 70ft (21 m) above the river: the builders had to muster all the skills of their craft to lock the final stones.

900 navvies were working on the line at the time. They were paid 5/- a day (25p). 'Drunk and riotous' offences, heard before Betws-y-coed Magistrates, soared to record numbers. The Fish Inn, still seen at the foot of the viaduct, opened at 6 a.m. The work was dangerous enough as it was, but amazingly, not a single life was lost during the construction of the viaduct. However, absenteeism was rife and in 1876, Gethin – according to local tradition – bought the pub and closed it. Work got under way much more efficiently afterwards! The ingenious viaduct was spontaneously named Pont Gethin by the locals. It has become the master builder's living memorial.

Pont Gethin – the railway viaduct crossing the Lledr valley

The Fish Inn, near Pont Gethin

Pont Gethin crossing the A470

Lead mining remains at Aberllyn, above Betws-y-coed

Hafodlas slate quarry, near Pentre-du

Mines, quarries and forests

Evidence of Roman leadmining has been found at Cae Mawr mine, near the Roman fort of Caer Llugwy. John Wynn of Gwydir (1553-1627) could probably be described however as the pioneer of the mining which took place on his estate in the mountainous terrain between Llanrwst and Tŷ Hyll. The lead ore won – a comparatively small quantity of about a hundred tons a year – was shipped from Trefriw Quay to smelters in Flintshire.

More capital and investment ensured that larger companies and more efficient machinery were used and by 1900 over five hundred miners worked underground, living in the back streets of Llanrwst and the mining village of Pentre-du in Betws-y-coed. The nearest mines to Betws-y-coed were Aberllyn (in the gorge under Llyn Parc), Coed Mawr Pool and Cyffty (across Afon Llugwy from Pentre-du). Mining continued in the Parc Mine until the 1950s.

The mountains of Eryri are also rich in slate veins. Large quarries were worked in Cwm Penmachno and around Dolwyddelan. Nearer Betws-y-coed, one of the largest quarries was Hafodlas, near Pentre-du. It opened in the 1850s and produced mostly slab slates – raising production to over 2,000 tonnes per annum by 1900. Over 50 quarrymen worked here and a tramway to Betws-y-coed station was planned but never built. The substantial platform at Betws-y-coed is still referred to as Cei Llechi ('*slate quay*') from the time it was a transit point for slates.

Up to the 1940's, a community of smallholders lived at Rhiwddolion, now a deserted village on the old Roman road beyond Pentre-du. The men lived off their small fields and worked in local mines and quarries – they got up at 5 a.m. and walked to Pont-y-pant station to catch the train to start work in the Blaenau Ffestiniog mines at 7 a.m. The community had a shop and chapel, which doubled up as a school during weekdays. The schoolmaster at one time was Gutyn Arfon, composer of the well-known Welsh hymntune 'Llef'. Rhiwddolion chapel was the first in

Caernarfonshire to allow a musical instrument inside its walls – a harmonium was carried there by trap and pony.

The community dispersed in the great depression of the early 1930's when the slate quarries of Ffestiniog felt the squeeze. Only the ruins and old fruit trees remain – still flowering and bearing apples in neglected orchards.

In 1921, the Forestry Commission started planting around Betws-y-coed, what was to become one of the largest forests in Wales, providing employment to plug the gap left by other declining industries. Coed Gwydir spans the slopes from Dolgarrog to Cwm Penmachno and lines of spruce, larch and pine have dislodged the native oak, beech and ash. After the initial mistakes, more care is taken today to sustain a slightly better ecological balance. There are 100 miles of forestry roads in Coed Gwydir with many picnic spots, offering excellent facilities to walkers and mountain bikers alike.

Rhiwddolion

Cyffty mine in the Gwydir forest

A picinic area in the forest

Tŷ Hyll

Tŷ Hyll – details

From crafts to craft shops

Cyfraith Hywel Dda – the old Welsh legal code which served the needs of the nation for over six centuries – deemed that he who built a house between sunset and sunrise, complete with walls, roof and a smoking chimney, could live in it and claim it as freehold together with the land from the four corners of the house measured by the throw of an axe. It was known as a 'tŷ unnos' (*one-night house*) and this was how small crofts first sprung up on the woodlands above Betws-y-coed. A unique reminder of this period is found above Rhaeadr Ewynnol on a sharp bend in the A5. It is called Tŷ Hyll.

The rugged cottage has been translated as 'ugly house' – hardly an accurate description, certainly not in the eyes of its numerous visitors, who come year in year out to soak up the old-world atmosphere, and to hear about Cymdeithas Eryri (*Snowdonia*

A riverside walk near Tŷ Hyll

Society) who endeavour to safeguard the culture and landscape of Eryri. Some of the stones weigh three and a half tons and how they were put in place is a miracle of engineering – but Wales is a land of stone and Welshmen have an uncanny ability to handle enormous stones with the most basic of implements.

According to local legend, it was built by two outlawed brothers. Later, Irish drovers used it and navvies working on Telford's new road lodged in it. It has been a visitor's attraction since the mid 19th century. The old cottage has seen all that has passed on the road for centuries and is now as pleasant as ever, the interior and garden recently restored.

It would serve well as a pattern. Betws-y-coed has continually guarded its rich Welsh past and its outstanding natural beauty against inappropriate developments. Accommodation is plentiful, from caravan parks to rented rooms to highly recommended hotels. It is an ideal base from which to explore all the main

The visitor centre at Royal Oak stables

There is a wide selection of hotels and guest houses at Betws-y-coed

Craig Forys hilltop is reached by a track through the forest

Plas y Brenin outdoor activities centre, Capel Curig

attractions of northern Wales.

The area is bustling with natural resources that offer a great variety of adventures to the outdoor person. This is all-weather walking country, from the excellent variety of paths ideal for riverside, lakeside and woddland walks to the more adventurous Snowdonia mountain rambles. Some of the best mountain bike tracks in Wales are found in the nearby forests, while general cycling is a pastime enjoyed by more and more people on the quieter roads and bike routes.

A forestry parking/picnic area

Bike hiring facilities at Betws

A riverside artist

Just outside Betws-y-coed, the Tree Tops offers outdoor activities at a unique high ropes centre available to wide range of customers. Open 7 days a week with visitor centre, licenced bar and cafe, showers, car park (www.ttadventure.co.uk).

At the village, the outdoor activity shops now offer good reliable equipment for the hundreds of ramblers, mountaineers, campers, bikers and wild-water enthusiasts who come to these valleys every year.

The Tree Tops rope adventure centre

The shopping centres at Royal Oak stables and the station square

Galleries and local craft and produce shops on the main street

There are plenty of interesting things to do to without leaving the village. The visitor centre in the old Royal Oak Stables (*www.visitsnowdonia.info*), with its craft workshops and mountain bike hire, is an attraction in itself. Nearby the motor museum and the railway museum collections and memorabilia conjure up a golden age. There is also a miniature train ride for children. There are plenty of galleries and pottery workshops to drop in on nearby. A few miles up the Llugwy valley, canoeing, skiing, wall climbing and all kinds of highland adventures are on offer at the Plas y Brenin national mountain centre.

Whatever your fancy, Betws-y-coed will offer something different for you to take back home, and you can be confident that its unique Welsh characteristics will be there to welcome you when you return.

The railway museum near the Conwy Valley line at Betws

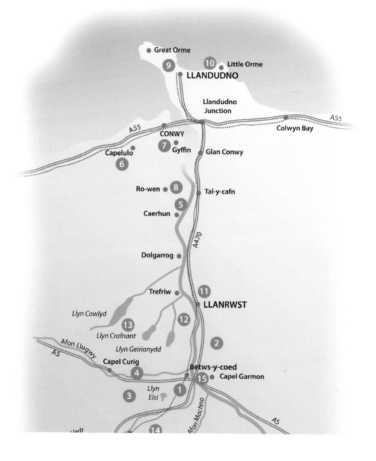

A Walk around Betws-y-coed
The Church to Llyn Elsi

Walk details

Approx distance: *4 miles/6.4 kilometres*

Approx time: *3-3½ hours*

O.S. Maps: *1:50 000 Landranger Sheet 115*
1:25 000 Explorer OL 17

Start: *Station car park, Betws-y-coed.*
Grid Ref. SH 795 566

Access: *Minor road past the church at Betws-y-coed.*

Parking: *Car park by the rail station.*

Going: *Riverside and woodland paths.*

Walk directions

1. From the car park, cross the A5 and turn right towards the church. Turn off the main road and follow a minor road round behind the church to where a track leading up into the woods will be found, passing a barrier on the way next to the information board. Note the blue and white-topped marker post. Continue up the stony track, passing another such post and on to cross a stream by a seat and a sign to Llyn Elsi. Continue up past more posts to where the track forks. Take the right fork marked by a white-topped post. This leads to a T-junction where you turn right as marked by a white-topped post.
At the next junction bear left uphill (white post) and then right

at the following junction (white post). Continue up to another T-junction and follow the white post to the left, which leads to Llyn Elsi.

2. At the lakeside, turn back to the right, with the lake on your left, along a narrow path (white post) and continue up to a viewing point overlooking the lake with a stone plinth on the

summit. Now ignore the path marked by the white post and take the path to the left passing the end of the lake, and follow it to the small dam. Do not cross the wooden bridge but turn right along a path parallel to the stream. This soon meets a stone road. Now turn left along the road. At a junction marked 'Hafod Las', keep left along the main track and then bear right at the next junction. Continue along this designated cycleway passing where another road enters from the left. Keep to this main forestry road, passing on to more open country and follow the 'S' bends downhill. You will pass a view into the valley to the west of Betws-y-coed and see the A5 road in the bottom. Continue round the hillside and on down the stone road to a junction under some power cables.

Bear right and follow the main track downhill to where it will eventually meet the A5 road.

3. Cross the road to the footpath and turn left. Soon you will come to a gap in the wall with a wooden barrier. Take this path down to the river and swing right along the river bank by the old house ruins, following it downstream through Artist's

78

Wood. Continue along this path, rough in places, crossing a wooden bridge to the Miner's Bridge. It is not immediately spotted, but is opposite a lone house on the A5 to your right. The path swings left and down some steps to the river.

4. Cross the bridge, which in itself is a steep climb, and turn right along the opposite bank still following the river downstream. The path will cross a ladder stile into an open riverside field and then become woods again. Continue until you come to Pont-y-pair. This you cross and turn left along the A5 through Betws-y-coed to the car park.

Walk selected from:

Carreg Gwalch Best Walks in the Conwy Valley

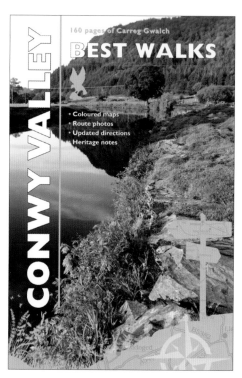

Also in the series:

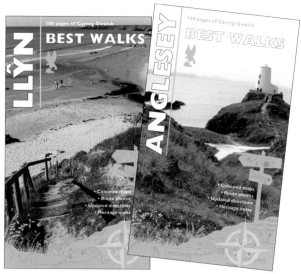